pillars of the Church

supporting chaplaincy in
further and higher education

⊕ CHURCH HOUSE
PUBLISHING

Church House Publishing
Church House
Great Smith Street
London
SW1P 3NZ

ISBN 0 7151 9046 6

Cover design by
Church House Publishing
Typeset in 9/11
Printed by Halstan & Co. Ltd.
Amersham, Bucks

Published 2002 for the Board of
Education of the Archbishops'
Council by Church House Publishing

*Copyright © The Archbishops' Council
2002*

GS Misc 667

All rights reserved. No part of this
publication may be reproduced or
stored or transmitted by any means
or in any form, electronic or
mechanical, including photocopying,
recording, or any information storage
and retrieval system, without written
permission which should be sought
from the Copyright and Contracts
Administrator, The Archbishops'
Council, Church House, Great Smith
Street, London SWIP 3NZ.

Tel: 020 7898 1557
Fax: 020 7898 1449
copyright@c-of-e.org.uk

*This report has only the authority
of the Board that produced it.*

contents

preface	v
introduction	vii
findings	viii
conclusions and recommendations	x
acknowledgements and abbreviations	xii
section 1 further education	1
working with further education and the learning and skills sector – guidelines for the Church	1
introduction	1
how the local church relates to the sector	3
some examples of practice	7
some issues needing further attention	11
section 2 higher education	14
introduction	14
reflecting on higher education chaplaincy ministry	14
issues	16
diocesan structures	21
questions of practice	23
one question	31
appendix 1	
background to the consultation process	32
appendix 2	
original letter and responses to enquiry	33
notes	36
index	41

preface

Each day, chaplains are at work in colleges and universities across the land. Their core ministry brings the Church into direct contact with many people who would never venture inside a church building.

In recent years, further and higher education has fundamentally changed and now offers a range of student experiences largely unimagined by those of us whose student days are long passed. These changes are far-reaching, including structure and funding, and have affected staff as well as students. Moreover, the recent expansion is set to continue and challenge traditional ways of providing education. Chaplains in the midst of this have been supporting people, both Church members and those outside the Church's life.

This report provides a snapshot of pressing issues, both in education itself and for the Church within it. Its context was an enquiry into the range of diocesan practice. Six regional consultation days were held. I am grateful to all who participated, whether chaplains, staff, ecumenical partners, bishops or diocesan officers, and to Anthea Turner and Paul Brice, the Board of Education officers for further and higher education. It was time well spent, and much enthusiasm and commitment was expressed in discussing this important aspect of the Church's ministry.

It is my hope that this report will further strategic thinking as the Church seeks to engage with the people creating our future.

✠ Alan Blackburn
Chairman, Board of Education

introduction

1 Huge changes have occurred in the nation's education and vision in the last ten years. The changes impact on everyone[1] and are likely to continue. These changes have affected institutions, staff, students and their families alike, and the nation as a whole (including employers, and the financial sector), as well as there being new expectations of the Church.[2]

2 Those directly concerned have been grappling with the implications of these changes, whether staff or chaplains, often in isolation. There is currently a need for society, and the Church in particular, to catch up[3] and take stock of these changes, from which no one is immune.

3 The consultation by the Board of Education's Further and Higher Education Committee originated from a letter to dioceses requesting information about chaplaincy support. The resulting picture gleaned from this exercise showed that diocesan support was most varied and sometimes patchy. Hence this attempt to bring the issues to the fore and facilitate wider attention being paid to them.

4 Further and higher education will be detailed separately as many dioceses deal with them independently. Where, in a number of dioceses, they share an education committee, the common issues may be addressed with appropriate overlap. It is hoped that some joined-up thinking will be done by dioceses both between further and higher education, and also between further/higher education and other areas of work. In fact we would encourage this at diocesan strategy level.

findings

1 Principals, vice-chancellors and their staff often value the different perspective a chaplain can offer in thinking about educational change, their institution's responses, values and well-being.

2 Chaplaincy is generally welcomed as a legitimate contribution to institutional and individual well-being. It is sometimes endorsed by being included in some manner in formal inspections (TQA, RAE, QAA, OFSTED, ALI). However, institutional attitudes to chaplaincy vary, often depending on its contextual development or the mind-set of senior college personnel. Healthy relations between institution and Church can be encouraged by informed interaction with a diocese at civic and senior levels, taking note of regional developments.

3 There is a need for dioceses to establish and maintain on-going support, monitoring and partnership with chaplaincy as it ministers in continually changing sectors.

Chaplaincy situations are so varied that there can be no universal blueprint, but some clear principles did emerge:

(i) good **structure**, adequate **resourcing**, plus clear channels of formal **communication**, **accountability** and **support** are prerequisite for chaplaincy, and
(ii) in particular, the importance of establishing a small core of dedicated individuals to drive the chaplaincy agenda within a diocese.[1]

4 Chaplaincy is at the cutting edge of mission, discerning the presence of God in daily life and finding a new language in which to explore key issues with non-churchgoers of all ages. This can strip away many assumptions of priestly formation, training and practice if it has been too parochially determined. Consequently:

a) Involvement with chaplaincy can be a valuable context for professional development, and exploring afresh the nature of ministry.[2]
b) It is hoped that one outcome of this consultation would be some interaction between chaplains and theological training colleges.[3]
c) The starkness of huge institutions now calls for capable individuals and teams with great commitment and stamina, as well as creativity.

d) The temptation still lies to recreate parochialisms to retreat into, instead of facing the challenge of new ways of reaching out and being.

Nevertheless, it is still important for full-time (often higher education) chaplains to have an appropriate spiritual base to feed and support their ministry. Crucially this must avoid adding inappropriate parochial/diocesan demands that detract from, rather than add force to, a vigorous chaplaincy-focus. In the context of part-time (often further education) chaplaincy, active diocesan encouragement needs to be given to sharing the experience gained from partnership in the community, between college and parish.

5 Chaplains often felt misunderstood both by people in the institution they serve and the church that sends them.

a) Institution – chaplaincy does not fit easily into college structures and squeezing it into such (e.g. student support) may lose something of critical importance.

b) Church – in the Church, such misunderstanding is often due to outdated views of a now greatly changed education structure.

6 Theological reflection by chaplains across the nation is always taking place, especially at the annual conferences. However, this accumulated wisdom is analogous to an *oral tradition* of the sector, passed down among their number not unlike the Early Church. This does not necessarily help those chaplains/clergy who are unable, unwilling or not resourced to attend national conferences, nor members of the Church seeking to understand the issues. (Diocesan staff have been invited to conference in the past, but few have taken up such opportunities.)

a) Chaplains are now aware of and eager to redress this.

b) Theological expression of chaplaincy experience needs to be encouraged from a range of current practitioners, particularly those well informed by their breadth of experience and activity in the national network.

c) Fundamental questions arose in the consultation about mission as a whole, especially in response to such matters as: mission and workplace chaplaincy, the nature of the Church, and changing patterns of leisure and study.

d) Interacting and thinking with academics is a key element of ministry exercised by chaplains, not usually available to any extent in a parish.

conclusions and recommendations

1 The Church, in all its dioceses, must be clear about the priority of education chaplaincy in its mission to the nation.

. . . that each diocese clarify the focus of educational chaplaincy ministry in its diocesan vision.

2 One-third of young adults pass through higher education and an equally significant proportion of the population through further education, making education an accessible and legitimate context in which to interact with the population.

. . . that each diocese take encouragement from the openness towards education chaplains, within educational institutions rather than outside them, to engage with people 'where they are' in this challenging and kairos *context.*

3 If the Church is to have any germane contact with those beyond its walls, education is the natural context in which the issues of life and purpose arise.

. . . that each diocese recognize the culture shift in society making the potential of a more natural encounter with faith at the work place, rather than the home space.

4 In particular, education is a place inhabited by significant people: the thinkers and creators of tomorrow.

. . . that each diocese take active steps in the professional development of clergy to address a) the issue of enabling of Church members to think critically with their faith within their academic specialism, but also b) how to engage with non-members about creating future society.

5 Not only has education changed but so too has the cultural context in which it is delivered.

. . . that each diocese offer opportunities for the Church to learn with chaplains about mission in the multi-faith context of education institutions and about the wider implications for parishes and the future ministry of the Church.

conclusions and recommendations

6 What is education saying to the Church? Inevitably the Church has to respond to the far-reaching changes in our education system and who, but its practitioners, chaplains and students, can relate this story?

. . . that each diocese consider how to encourage the awareness and debate of issues raised by education in its communications strategy, diocesan and parish magazines.

7 Clergy, congregations and ordinands have a part to play in thinking about and responding to what education is saying to the Church and reflecting on the issues.

. . . that each diocese, in its central structures and parishes, give opportunities for hearing and considering the issues raised by education, and support Church members engaged in it.

8 Chaplaincy, rather than being seen as a specialism on the margins, is a fundamental part of the normal ministry of the Church.

. . . that each diocese, along with theological training institutions, consider chaplaincy as a context and resource in which to explore future ministry.

9 Bishops and dioceses often have civic connections with major local educational institutions and can recognize the importance of this in their diocesan policy.

. . . that each diocese express its commitment to these institutions by implementing appropriate chaplaincy support and communication structures to make its presence effective.

The Revd Paul E P Brice
Secretary, Further and Higher Education Committee
Board of Education

acknowledgements and abbreviations

The publisher would like to thank the following for permission to reproduce copyright material:

Revd Tim Jenkins for extracts from the transcript of the chaplaincy video *Being there* (pp.38–9)

Revd Melanie Griffith for her response to the email query on support (p.38)

AEO	Adult Education Officer
ALI	Adult Learning Inspectorate
CMEO	Continuing Ministerial Education Officer
CTE	Churches Together in England
DBE	Diocesan Board of Education
DDE	Diocesan Director of Education
DYO	Diocesan Youth Officer
GNVQ	General National Vocational Qualification
LEA	Local Education Authority
LSC	Learning and Skills Council
MARCEA	Merseyside and Region Churches' Ecumenical Association
NEAFE	National Ecumenical Agency in Further Education
OFSTED	Office for Standards in Education
QAA	Quality Assurance Agency for Higher Education
RAE	Research Assessment Exercise
TEC	Training Enterprise Council
TQA	Teaching Quality Assessment
UCCF	Universities and Colleges Christian Fellowship

section 1
further education

working with further education and the learning and skills sector – guidelines for the Church

introduction

1 The world of post-16 education and training is markedly different at the start of the twenty-first century from even a decade ago. In 1993, FE colleges became independent corporations, driven to review the contemporary relevance of their curricula in context, and to ensure high quality service with relatively scarce resources.

2 Now, since 2001, the creation of the Learning and Skills Council brings under one umbrella strategic planning and resourcing for both education and training post-16 (traditionally seen in this country to have been entirely separate entities), along with adult and community lifelong learning. The Learning and Skills Council (LSC) funds all categories, except higher education in the universities, wherever learning takes place.

3 Thus, the new learning and skills sector with its four million students might be seen as a microcosm of local communities, covering a very broad age, social, ethnic and ability range, and offering the widest curriculum from basic skills through to degrees.

- For instance, did you know that there are more full-time 16- and 17-year-old students in further education than in schools, and more students in further education than in the universities?
- Did you know that FE colleges provide more higher education today than was offered in the whole university sector at the time of the Robbins Report in the 1960s, and that they provide a substantial proportion of new entrants to degree courses?
- FE colleges, moreover, are the most important single provider of skills into the economy, delivering 49 per cent of all vocational qualifications achieved in the UK, including 66 per cent of those at level 3.

4 The term 'technical college' has largely fallen out of use since, although colleges still teach engineering and construction, the changing needs of the economy have created demand for business studies, and preparation for work in the service industries and caring professions. At the same time, there has been a great increase in college provision for the humanities and social sciences, often for adults wishing to move into higher education.

5   It may be helpful at this stage to differentiate more clearly between the categories of work undertaken by FE colleges. Churches might want to reflect on the gaps in their current support:

- 16–18-year-olds full-time.
- Adults full-time and part-time. Programmes are increasingly modularized, allowing people to spend varying times of their learning week in college, and allowing them to spread their learning over differing periods. The distinction between vocational and recreational learning is also not always clear, often being in the mind of the learner rather than intrinsic to the programme's design. Sometimes colleges have managed the local Adult and Community Education Service, whereas in other areas a freestanding service has run alongside equivalent college provision.
- Workforce development. This includes both modern apprenticeships, and also the updating, retraining and certification of older people who are already fully employed. Much of this work requires the active collaboration of employers, and some of it will probably take place in the workplace. This is likely to be an area of very considerable growth during the next few years.
- Employability, which includes important areas of work such as New Deal provision, basic skills, courses for refugees and so on.
- The volume of higher education taking place in FE colleges will further increase with the advent of two-year Foundation degrees, which are vocationally-orientated and – although under the aegis of a university – will be partly delivered in colleges.

6   Consequently, it is not surprising that, despite the diversity of providers, FE colleges (by virtue of their location, community outreach, experience, quality and long-standing networks of relationships) are key players in post-16 education, training and lifelong learning.

7   Colleges share much common ground with the Church, in their commitment to the worth of all individuals, the development of given skills to their full potential, the valuing of work (broadly understood), and their responsiveness to the needs of the communities they serve.

8 They are closely integrated with regional economic and social planning, and tasked with major responsibilities in terms of urban and rural regeneration, and neighbourhood renewal. They are seen as having key roles to play in terms of developing a strong economy and a vibrant, inclusive society.

9 Local people, however, see the college as 'their' college, and to a significant degree see its role as equipping them for, and supporting them through, transition – such as returning to learning after a gap, or gaining new skills for a change in direction at work, or achieving the necessary qualifications for employment. At such times in a person's life, when serious thought is being given to matters of personal worth, identity and purpose, there is a real pastoral role for the Church – that is, to offer solidarity and support. Moreover, the formation of future leaders in business, industry and society is an area in which the Church has a vital role to play.

10 Given this common ground, and recognizing the changing context, the Church may wish to strengthen its engagement with further education – still the Cinderella in a Church context, which has found it simpler to relate to schools and higher education. The Church of England and Methodist Church together jointly fund a national officer (The Churches' National Adviser in Further Education), who is happy to offer guidance and support. For example, help is available on job descriptions, appointment procedures, induction, training, continuing development, appraisal, and structural support at local level. The Roman Catholic Church has a Lifelong Learning Officer, from whom information about their 16 sixth-form colleges may be obtained. The National Ecumenical Agency in Further Education (NEAFE) has recently been restructured, chaired by the Chief Executive of the University for Industry, with senior clergy from three denominations as its joint vice-chairs and strong representation from across the sector. Nevertheless, at regional and local levels, the sector has relatively few recognized links with the Church. This is a timely moment to refocus on the Church's engagement with the world, the economy and its institutions and people.

how the local church relates to the sector
the congregation

11 Since further education is where many local people learn, it is likely that every church will have some contact, whether recognized or not. One of the 450 FE colleges (general, sixth-form college, land-based or specialist) or one of its outreach learning centres, will probably be located in the area. Members of the congregation and local community (both young and older) will be attending a nearby college as learners, or using its distance-learning facilities. Local public and private sector employers will be working with the college to update the skills of their workforce.

12 A wide range of voluntary and community organizations will be in partnership with the college, contributing to a variety of programmes. An increasing number of local churches are actively engaged themselves in this process, particularly in the context of the Government's widening participation, social inclusion, citizenship, New Deal, Connexions, adult basic skills and information technology agendas, often running classes on the premises, or offering placements. Church members, through their involvement in voluntary service, may well be working on schemes funded by the colleges and Learning and Skills Council.

13 The Churches' Beacon Award for Sustainable Community Development, one of a prestigious series of national awards within the sector, administered by further education's Association of Colleges, recognizes excellent work in this field. Further education chaplains, at the interface between the college, the local church and community, often have a significant contribution to make here.

14 Since April 2001, OFSTED has taken on responsibility for the inspection of all 16–18 full-time education in colleges as well as schools, whereas the new Adult Learning Inspectorate covers all other post-16 categories except higher education. Both inspectorates, led by OFSTED, will also undertake area inspections of all provision in the locality. Christian college staff, employers and community workers, whether providing learning in colleges, the workplace, or local community premises, will want to affirm the importance of high quality, and work to ensure its effective recognition.

the clergy

15 Some local clergy, or members of their congregations, already offer some form of chaplaincy to their college – generally part-time, though a few colleges contribute to the funding of a full-time chaplaincy. Over 200 FE colleges have such contact, and there is increasing college interest in developing these links.

16 In most cases, the chaplains' work with the colleges is but one small element of a much broader Church ministry. Without question, their witness is at the cutting edge of mission, discerning the presence of

God in daily life and finding a new language in which to explore key issues of life and death, meaning and purpose, with non-churchgoers of all ages. Interestingly, FE colleges have made a significant contribution to the Church's understanding of 'spirituality'.

17 Clearly, this challenging task is one which is best supported at diocesan level, and integrated into diocesan strategic planning, rather than being seen as an optional extra at parochial level, dependent on the particular interest of an individual. Crucially, the colleges look for sustained Church commitment. Early discussion between key partners to agree priorities is crucial, and supports the building of a sound relationship.

18 Further education chaplaincy is frequently provided ecumenically. Chaplaincies currently include the following denominations: Church of England, Roman Catholic, Methodist, Baptist, United Reformed, Church of Scotland, Salvation Army, Quaker, Pentecostal and others. Colleges particularly value chaplaincy on an ecumenical, or multi-faith, basis, looking to the Church to support their own emphasis on the development of an inclusive society, which values and respects diversity. Some significant pioneering work has been done by further education chaplains in this important area. Such joint local ventures offer a valuable form of witness, as much to the Church as to the college, and can help to develop an understanding of ecumenism at its best. Effective working on the ground needs, however, to be integrated into denominational structures so that, for instance, issues of accountability are properly addressed.

19 What, then, do further education chaplains do? The nature of their work will vary considerably, depending on the focus agreed with the college, their particular personal gifts and experience and, of course, the time they are able to offer to the college. Typically, they will be seen as:

- offering pastoral support to staff and students;
- contributing to the wider community's understanding of the sector;
- offering an independent and balanced perspective on policy and action;
- helping to make explicit the values and ethical dimensions which underpin the curriculum;
- exploring issues related to work, human identity, citizenship and worth;
- helping to facilitate inter-faith dialogue;
- contributing to the life of the whole college through voluntary

activities, corporate events and the provision of opportunities for worship, celebration and reflection.

The chaplain may also provide a link back into the local church: there are small Christian Unions, linked to UCCF, in a quarter of the colleges and local churches support them by providing speakers and resources or venues for shared meetings.

20   A chaplain may be invited to serve as governor on the college corporation, or other appropriate policy-making groups, such as its equal opportunities, or inclusive learning committees.

21   Clearly, the more regular the commitment to the college, the better equipped the chaplain is to make an effective contribution.

22   Effective further education chaplains have brought different kinds of experience – some have a youth and community background, others industrial, hospital or prison chaplaincy, others their previous business or commercial backgrounds and, equally importantly, others as local clergy have a strong pastoral understanding of their local community. Churches might want to consider the extent to which involvement in further education chaplaincy provides opportunity for a helpful shift in focus – a revitalizing contact with contemporary secular culture. Many chaplains bring another dimension of awareness, and expertise, to the work and thinking of local churches. The involvement of the 'right' person is vital – someone who is prepared to meet people where they are, with a willingness to listen, to learn from and relate to people, along with a clear sense of Christian service. Style and energy are more important than age.

the college staff

23   It is most important not to underestimate the degree to which Christian college staff themselves may already be offering a form of unrecognized 'chaplaincy', affirmed more readily by the college than recognized by the local church. There are important connections to be made here with the effective development of the Church's understanding of, and support to, lay discipleship and lay ministry.

24   For instance, there are a good number of staff (teaching and non-teaching) and managers in further education, whose work is informed by Christian values and who strive to ensure that 'life in all its fullness' becomes a reality in the ethos of the whole college, in learners' experience, and in the ways in which people are treated within the workplace. Whether through the exploration of economic, social and ethical issues in business, health and social care,

information technology, engineering and catering, or community-based adult education, or tutor training, there is a good deal of Christian witness taking place.

25 This work is, to a large extent, divorced from the Church-produced resource material, which is more naturally circulated to schools than to colleges. Church adult, youth and social responsibility teams, along with regional theological centres, may want to consider whether there are ways in which their experience and resources might usefully be shared more widely.

some examples of practice

Given the diversity of approaches to the learning and skills sector across the Churches, a representative sample is provided here, to generate thinking. Further information may be obtained from Anthea Turner, Churches' National Adviser in Further Education. Additional examples are always welcomed!

structures

26 It is helpful when someone with senior responsibility in the diocese (or equivalent) has an understanding of further education. For instance, the Bishops of Blackburn and Stafford have both served as FE college governors. The diocesan directors of education in Canterbury, Durham and Coventry have experience of working with further education. The Archdeacon of Wakefield has a brief to support further education, as does the Archdeacon of Surrey who, until recently, chaired the Church of England's Further and Higher Education Committee. Two of the four Methodist Connexional Coordinating Secretaries have worked in further education.

27 Synod members with experience of further education are able to make a most valuable contribution at local and national levels.

28 The following areas are currently represented in the National Further Education Officers' Advisory Network: Bath and Wells, Bristol, Gloucester and Salisbury, Chelmsford, Exeter, Guildford, Lancashire, Lincolnshire, Manchester, Merseyside, Oxford, Portsmouth, Southwark, Southwell, and the West Midlands. Some further education officers combine the role with chaplaincy to a college, others are recently retired senior college staff. For instance, Guildford Diocese has a recently retired college principal as its further education adviser.

29 Ecumenical networks oversee chaplaincy in Merseyside (MARCEA), Manchester (CTE) and Lincolnshire (CTE).

30 Southwell Diocese has a recently retired further education principal on its Board of Education.

31 Cambridge Regional College has active links with the East of England Churches' Forum.

32 Several dioceses, including Leicester, have a diocesan further education policy.

33 The West Midlands churches ecumenically, under the aegis of St Peter's Saltley Trust, have appointed two further education development workers, with a specific brief to build on the work of their earlier five field officers, who linked with all FE colleges in the region. From that earlier base, it is now possible to do some in-depth work at local level, the results of which will be widely disseminated.

34 Canterbury and Rochester Dioceses work together to ensure an active further and higher education committee, which has organized several successful events.

35 Worcester Diocese has reorganized its post-16 work under a newly created tertiary committee.

36 Both Winchester and Oxford Dioceses commissioned further education chaplains to audit the churches' links with all the local colleges, and advise on future development.

37 Trinity Theological College, Bristol arranged a half-day a week theological student placement at an FE college.

38 Derby Diocese has developed further education chaplaincy through its higher education associated colleges network.

39 Some churches work through a sympathetic 'lead' college in the area.

communications

40 Lincolnshire CTE supports a full-time chaplain (paid for by the diocese) at North Lindsey College and John Leggott sixth-form college, who sees it as a major part of the job to keep further education in the public eye in the Church. This is achieved by mailing an annual report widely, writing articles for the diocesan magazine, organizing an annual chaplaincy open event/lecture, preaching and talking about further education across the area, and co-editing a

magazine called *HighliFE*. Similarly, the full-time chaplain at Grimsby College and Franklin sixth-form college produces full reports that are widely circulated.

41 The south-west dioceses, with the support of St Matthias Trust, have produced a glossy newspaper – *FEatures* – capable of wide circulation in the Church, and very well received in the sector. Some dioceses, and others, have indicated their willingness to sponsor pages for a future edition.

42 Southwark Diocese has produced a leaflet, identifying all its colleges and the support offered by the Church. This follows a further education research project, sponsored by the diocese.

43 Bournemouth and Poole FE college chaplain produced a video about chaplaincy with the help of the college's GNVQ media students, as part of their curriculum assignment. His further education chaplain's 'diary' – an account of his experiences over a number of years working at the college – now features on the Trinity Theological College website.

44 Guildford's diocesan further education adviser circulates a regular update to colleges and chaplains.

45 Many college chaplains, e.g. Bracknell, Loughborough, Stafford, Weymouth, Grimsby and North Lindsey, produce leaflets about the chaplaincy, as part of the student services provision.

church/college events

46 The Bishop of Hereford hosted a half-day seminar for colleges, churches, voluntary organizations and LEAs on 'Lifelong learning: church and state'.

47 Portsmouth and Newcastle Dioceses hosted events for college senior managers to explore the implications of the Churches' publication 'Developing a spirituality policy in FE sector colleges'.

48 Cambridgeshire college chaplains and staff have an active post-16 spirituality group, which has produced a values statement.

49 The Bishop of Bath and Wells invited college principals to dinner at the bishop's palace, to discuss matters of shared interest.

50 CTE in Lincolnshire hosted an event for churches, colleges, TECs, careers companies and voluntary organizations to explore the implications of the Connexions youth support strategy.

pillars of the Church

51 St Peter's Saltley Trust hosts regular seminars for colleges and church leaders in the West Midlands.

52 Guildford Diocese runs training events for college managers and staff, with a particular focus on curriculum and college management, and the bishop spoke at a diocesan conference for college principals.

53 Manchester and Stockport Methodist District synod was held in an FE college, and information technology training was offered to clergy.

54 Leicester Diocese hosted annual further education dinners, with an external speaker, using college-catering restaurants.

55 The chaplain at Myerscough College has facilitated joint Church/college support to the farming community in the recent foot and mouth epidemic.

56 Drama students from Blackburn College participated in a Good Friday enactment at Blackburn Cathedral.

57 The Chelmsford further/higher education chaplains' diocesan retreat was addressed by a member of the college senior management team on the pastoral needs of students and staff.

community partnerships

58 The churches publicize all colleges shortlisted for the Churches' Beacon Award for Sustainable Community Development. To date, these have included the winners, Dunstable College, Stoke-on-Trent College and Loreto College, along with City of Sunderland, Woolwich, Harrogate, Hugh Baird Bootle, Broxtowe, Newcastle-under-Lyme and West Suffolk Colleges.

59 A further education chaplain sits on the Berkshire Local Learning and Skills Council, and the Bristol Diocese is represented on the Wiltshire and Swindon LSC.

60 Church members and leaders are involved in a developing number of Local Learning Partnerships, for instance in Merseyside and Wakefield, working with the Local Learning and Skills Councils, often on particular issues:

- Methodist and Anglican further education chaplains are working with Kent Learning Partnership in developing post-16 citizenship;
- the further education chaplain at Grimsby facilitates MPs' surgeries at the college.

multi-faith chaplaincy

61 Examples of active and effective multi-faith chaplaincies can be found at Suffolk College, Manchester College of Arts and Technology and Bourneville College, Birmingham.

62 St George's sixth-form centre, linked with City College Birmingham, has a multi-faith worship centre, and Grimsby College has a specially designated worship room.

63 The Chelmsford further education officer attends meetings of the inter-faith committee at Newham College.

chaplaincy support

64 Some churches regularly send their staff, and interested lay people, to national training conferences for further education.

65 Some churches expect and encourage annual reports from their further education chaplains. In most cases, these are the same dioceses that offer an effective support group.

66 Guildford Diocese is currently producing guidelines for good practice, and holds termly meetings for all chaplains.

67 Chelmsford Diocese has a prayer support group for further/higher education chaplains.

some issues needing further attention

need for an integrated strategy

68 What are the most effective ways of dioceses, and ecumenical partners, making links with regions (skills planning), Local Learning and Skills Councils (learning plans and budgets), Connexions Partnerships (youth support), and Local Strategic Partnerships (urban and rural regeneration, and neighbourhood renewal)? All of these are a challenge to Church structures, but are central to the effective implementation of so much of our work! FE colleges are intimately involved in all these areas.

69 What links already exist – as official representatives of the Church, or as lay members? How are they supported?

70 At what point do these structures impinge on the current, or proposed, work of diocesan and suffragan bishops, diocesan secretaries, archdeacons, area and rural deans, parish priests,

Boards of Education, Social Responsibility, Mission, Training . . . and their denominational equivalents?

71 There is a real need for joint planning at a senior level within the college and Church to secure a properly resourced chaplaincy. Colleges which have valued an effective chaplaincy feel betrayed when the Church fails to ensure a successor, particularly in view of the Church's tendency in the past to berate further education for its lack of interest. Too often this problem is identified far too late for action, causing unnecessary frustration.

72 The existence of the further education sector is rarely mentioned in parish profiles, or even in synod directories.

73 How can we more effectively harness the different, but valuable, skills of church youth, adult and community workers, in cooperation with further education staff, to meet the diverse challenges of contemporary society? Could we make better use of diocesan retreat houses?

what structures are in place for effective support and accountability?

74 Chaplains operate in exposed positions, both within the Church and the college, playing a key role often at times of crisis, and building bridges between the Church and the wider community. Effective support is vital.

75 How can we avoid problems of 'burn-out', caused by overloading capable and willing part-timers with too many ill-defined roles? What is understood by half-time, part-time, half-day chaplaincy? How can we avoid unnecessarily exposing chaplains to conflicting pressures between local church and chaplaincy?

76 Too often the Church's approach to supervision is amateur, compared to an increasingly professional approach within the sector. How does what is happening mesh with systems that are already operating in the Church and the college?

77 Is there a shared understanding of what constitutes effective chaplaincy? How would the college and Church measure 'success'? What evidence is looked for?

78 Support at national level can only be provided when dioceses and ecumenical partners ensure that records are kept up to date, and the centre informed of changes. It is very unfortunate if, because of that failure, chaplains and college staff are not included in central mailings.

79 Who needs to be on the chaplaincy advisory group?

ensuring willing and effective partnership

80 What is the most productive way of engaging with busy professionals, in the Church and sector? How can relationships and meetings be better focused, more relevant and timely?

81 How might we make better use of the further education sector's experience in offering high quality training – for instance, in management skills, information technology, counselling, media and so on?

There is certainly plenty of scope for creative thinking, and a climate in which fruitful dialogue may take place. If you wish to follow this up in any way, please contact:

Anthea Turner, Churches' National Adviser in Further Education, Church House, Great Smith Street, London, SW1P 3NZ.
Tel: 020 7898 1505. Email: anthea.turner@boe.c-of-e.org.uk

section 2
higher education

introduction

1 The Church at the beginning of the twenty-first century, like many other established organizations, is facing a period of change and uncertainty. This is nothing to be ashamed of or to evade. The world is changing at an increasing rate and other great institutions of our national heritage are also facing this, whether parliament, railways or health service; it is normal. At such times, however, specialist areas of ministry are prone to receiving less attention.

2 One of the changes of our time is the huge increase in the number of those engaged in higher education. Thus, with something over one-third of the population passing through higher education, this string to the Church's ministry bow is to be celebrated and focused.

3 Those taking part in the consultation, which included diocesan personnel not simply chaplains, were all emphatic that this ministry is vital to the Church.

4 This report calls for a strategic look at this specialist area of education ministry, because its importance remains, despite some dioceses being hard-pressed in time and personnel to think more broadly at this time.

5 It is good to be able to report that some dioceses and colleges are increasing their commitment to chaplaincy in response to the current growth of the sector and the increasing significance of the spiritual agenda within it.

reflecting on higher education chaplaincy ministry
a continuing process

6 The national education situation is constantly changing and this higher education report is simply a snapshot indicating the overall picture. Additional material on further and higher education sectors and their future will emerge in due course to continue the debate and development of ministry in them, and it is hoped that such material will be taken on-board by such diocesan bodies as further and higher education committees, chaplaincy management groups and the like:

- already, the letter, consultation and subsequent events have encouraged some dioceses to put their minds to chaplaincy development and support (some undertaking reviews), which is to be welcomed;
- it is hoped that the dioceses will feedback their experience and progress to the Board of Education to share practice;
- it is also hoped that they will take cognizance of this document, however recent their review, in the process of monitoring the implementation of their local recommendations, as the sectors are not static.

7 This constant movement in the sector demands that all dioceses participate in the process to monitor and respond:
- some dioceses have a long tradition of chaplaincy, but may need to review its practice and support;
- dioceses with new chaplaincy endeavours may or may not be well focused.

8 The world sets our agenda . . . go for it! (and let us know the results).

the Church's mission to the nation[1]

9 Mission is at the heart of chaplaincy. Its appropriate expression depends on each context due to local sensitivities. Mission, however, must be kept in mind when considering all the following sections.

10 Potential contact with people outside the Church, especially young adults but including all ages, many at a time of openness and learning, is now enormous, and the entrée for a chaplain probably far easier than in a parochial setting.

11 This concurs with a bishop's contribution on the importance of the Church ministering to people 'where they are', colleges and universities being 'an example par excellence'.

12 One contribution compared chaplains to missionaries in a foreign culture, in that they can be misunderstood by the sending body, having responded to local custom. What does this say to the Church about mission today? (Interestingly, Lord Dearing remarked that chaplains are missionaries at a previous Board of Education national conference.)

theological thinking on chaplaincy and beyond

For papers on chaplaincy from national conference, please see: http://www.cofe.anglican.org/about/education/hefe.html

Here follow some remarks made during the consultation:

13 Christianity is called to engage with the world for the sake of the kingdom in all places, not just in religious places. What is the nature of the engagement?

14 Chaplaincy derives from the historical role of the Church in learning communities, originally monastic communities, from which many colleges emerged. In contrast, how can the Church relate to the higher educational institutions of today?

15 In a prophetic role, chaplains can be a useful 'disrupting force', asking questions, often difficult ones, both of the Church and of their institution.

16 One chaplain remarked, 'Ground it in Gospel and the mission of the Church'. What does this mean in practice?

17 Promoting incarnation, of particular application in the context of higher education, is common to the parochial situation. This leads to the question, how does ministry across the whole Church avail itself to recent graduates whose experience of education and expectations of religion are very different nowadays?

issues
issues in higher education

18 *New meanings for higher education.* A vice-chancellor referred to colleges struggling with this. It is a challenge to institutions themselves, but also an opportunity for diocesan interaction with higher education leaders on the transmission of values and the wider purposes of education.

19 *The student is now seen as a paying consumer.* What are the implications of this customer-centred culture for education in general and as regards chaplaincy?

20 *There is structural change, but also a conceptual change* from elite to mass. There is also continuing debate in the sector about the nature and fundamentals of this change. This is a challenge to the Anglican Church in ministering to the nation, whose nature is changing:
- the fundamental structure of higher education has changed towards mass education provision;
- those employed in higher education are struggling to catch up with this sea-change;

- chaplains reported mouths wide open when speaking at the large numbers now in higher education;
- the student experience of the twenty-first century is now entirely different, exampled by much larger classes, less tutorial time, great financial pressure, part-time employment, e-learning, to name but a few;
- very few people participating in the consultation or reading this report will have been through a contemporary higher education experience;
- Church members too, as part of the population in general, do not realize the way higher education has changed drastically;
- even parents of current students often can't get to grips with how different the student experience is now, compared to their own, or even five years ago;
- we, the readers, all find it difficult to interpret the student experience except through our own distant memories of the same, the equivalent of which is now virtually extinct.

In what new ways can we attempt to understand the ivory towers we thought we already knew?

21 *Chaplaincy as a stakeholder in higher education*. Given that higher education has changed significantly and religious presence is more overt, how can the role of chaplaincy be developed for the future in partnership with institutions? Old models of ministry no longer apply and it is unwise to latch onto new models without going through the theological challenge and pain of developing a local approach to suit the particular situation. A long-time chaplain explained the notion of *continually* 'discovering' chaplaincy due to a never-ceasing process of learning to do ministry differently, rather than sticking with the mindset of a static model, which would limit their growth to embrace new challenges. A dynamic view of higher education ministry has to be held onto despite the unsettling that accompanies it.

issues for institutions

22 The ambiguity of chaplaincy, placed between the two differing institutions of Church and college, can be a creative tension. This can be used to advantage in ministry, but also presents a challenge, due to the assumptions or lack of understanding on either side:

- such ambiguity will not necessarily go away as the two institutions have different agendas and motivations;
- colleges can tend to box chaplaincy into student support or religious advisory role, legitimate aspects of chaplaincy, but most limiting as sole functions;

- there remains some difficulty in fitting chaplaincy into existing college structures.

23 There is a necessary role for challenging the purpose of a university, 'which no one is asking any more'. Are we, in higher education, supplying employable people, or citizens who ask questions?

24 Who can help an institution to understand its contact with the Church and its chaplains?

25 Overcoming the attitude of those who do not like the spirituality agenda is an ongoing issue. There is widespread goodwill towards chaplaincy but some academics are particularly sensitive and can cause ripples across the pond. How might existing goodwill be developed?

26 Other faith presence in higher education has become an increasingly important issue. It has also enabled the Christian presence in some institutions to be more public. How can the Church, with its historic experience in universities, assist institutions to understand the role religion has to play?

27 Partnership with universities in funding chaplaincy remains feasible, though sometimes sensitive. In an increasingly market-driven context, what is a proper balance of financial responsibility?

issues for consideration by dioceses

28 There is great diversity in both higher education and dioceses, and what works in one place may not in another, given local considerations. Institutions are not static either, and change may be required as the Church cannot rest on its laurels:

- a key point for emphasis is to keep discussion and support of chaplaincy and higher education on the boil, or at least simmering well: a small motivating group can be critical to achieving this;
- higher education is not as evenly spread across dioceses as further education. Some regional cooperation in addressing higher education issues may therefore be valuable;
- where diocesan attention to chaplaincy wanes, there lies potential danger for chaplain isolation and gradual devaluing or even diminishing of chaplaincy ministry in general;
- this is detrimental, as goodwill within institutions can be lost and may take considerable time to recover;
- far from being a reflection on chaplains, lack of goodwill may be an indicator of former diocesan neglect: who can redress this?

29 How can dioceses forge useful relationships with their local institutions? It was suggested that all higher education institutions need a senior diocesan official with higher education credibility who can reinforce the link between the Church and the institution and enhance the chaplain's formal presence. This would naturally be the bishop in most situations:

- how are bishops informed and enabled?
- how do they interact with chaplains?
- who else might be well-suited to this task?

30 It was evident that some bishops were in close contact with their chaplains and vice-chancellor(s) and this gave affirmation to the chaplain in the sight of senior college staff, enabling interaction as well as keeping the bishop informed of the education experience of large numbers of people in their diocese. As one bishop contributed, creating opportunities for diocesan dignitaries in their civic role was 'most important in oiling the mechanisms of the community at that level'. However, there were occasional examples of priests or bishops in contact with heads of institutions without appropriate briefing by, or consultation with, their chaplains, nor with briefing from others who had formal responsibility for ministry in the institutions. This was not thought to be good practice:

- It is valuable for bishops, in their civic role, to meet vice-chancellors and college principals, and affirm chaplains and chaplaincy ministry in the process. It is important for them to be briefed by the chaplains and make good use of every opportunity.
- Town/gown barriers are breaking down. Local community links with universities are now of utmost importance. A diocese can engage with this at diocesan, deanery, ecumenical, parochial and chaplaincy levels.

31 'It takes three years to work your way in', and any help getting up to speed is most useful. But learning for oneself is necessarily positive as well as unavoidable, especially in order to understand the intricacies of a specific institution. This does take time. Dioceses need to be aware and supportive during this period.

32 Chaplains can begin at a disadvantage. What thought is given to chaplaincy handover by a diocese?

33 In order to facilitate chaplaincy, support has to be effective and enabling, not bureaucratic and burdening.[2] Some sensitivity is therefore required in implementing changes to support that are positive, contributing towards improved ministry. This may demand

pillars of the Church

some creativity so as to avoid creating extra burdens both for the chaplain and for the diocese. Dioceses have to ask themselves the question, is there clarity over higher education support? (which applies to all its ministries).

34 In setting objectives, job descriptions must be realistic about the difficulties faced in part-time ministry, ministering to two universities or multi-site institutions, with being seen to be present.

35 One or two dioceses have combined chaplaincy posts with other posts. Sometimes arbitrarily rather than strategically. This has not enhanced chaplaincy ministry. A conference group debated this matter and concluded that a chaplain offering any less than three-quarters of their time in a university is unlikely to find acceptance as a participating member of an institution.

36 A wide variety of financial partnerships is in operation between Church and institutions. Debate took place on the value of chaplaincy independence enhancing ministry opportunity, being outside formal institutional structures. However, some chaplains, especially in a few 'new' universities, were very much a part of the college structure, with a line manager and review process, sometimes independent of the Church (this sometimes leads to other tensions). Our oldest colleges are similarly more independent of the Church in their management of chaplaincy.

37 Finance arrangements also impinge on the question of accountability. Who is a chaplain responsible to, and how helpful is this in practice? Most often, this would be the licensing bishop, but partnerships in funding may not produce the best practice in chaplain support if the resulting responsibility for support is too diffuse or confused. This issue may require addressing in some instances, paying proper regard to the chaplain's experience in practice.

issues for consideration by dioceses and their parishes

38 A broader agenda for dioceses is that clergy seem to vary enormously in their understanding of chaplaincy. Clergy and bishops, particularly those who have been chaplains in the past, may not realize the implications of the huge changes that have occurred in higher education in the last few years:
   - this impacts on the role of parish and local clergy in preparing their young for the college experience;
   - similarly, this impacts on ministry to recent graduates, whose different educational experience raises issues and expectations around worship, teaching and the fluidity of being church today;[3]

- chaplains could follow this up with diocesan communication departments.

39 Often, Christian staff in colleges are not involved in chaplaincy. This may have many reasons including parish commitments, pressure of time, commuting, reluctance, or ignorance of chaplaincy work. How can the Church engage and inform such members through its parishes?

40 Christian academics probably worship in their local parish rather than the chaplaincy. Are parishes facilitating such people to explore faith interaction in their field of study?

41 Applying Christian faith to one's work rather than at work, tends to be a weak area for Church members. The Christian faith is not content with simply being nice to people in the workplace. How can the Church as a whole promote contextual theology amongst all its members, specifically the academically gifted?

42 Christian academics can value the chaplain for discussing issues too difficult to raise in a parochial setting.

43 The Church has to recognize that the variety of ways of learning now is more pluriform than the ones in which it has traditionally been engaged.[4] How can the Church respond in order better to engage its members?

44 What can be learnt from chaplaincy about effective ministry to young graduates in parishes?

45 There is a wide spectrum of relationships between chaplaincies and student Christian societies, depending on the local context. Local churches and college staff can influence the quality of these relationships.

diocesan structures

46 This topic caused much discussion, which suggests that some specific work may be needed in this area. Diocesan structures are not similar. The wide-ranging ministry of dioceses can be subdivided very differently, some aspects emphasized and others effectively ignored. Higher education chaplaincy might be seen in one diocese as an education matter or in another as mission. Part of its work might overlap, to a limited extent, with adult education and youth work. Higher education chaplaincy sometimes falls outside a Board of Education's normal sphere of work, so who in a diocese is responsible for dealing with it locally and liaising with the national secretary/network? If dioceses place responsibility for chaplaincy outside the Board of Education, clarity is required in terms of diocesan liaison and structural placing of chaplains vis-à-vis national bodies. Day-to-day this can affect simple matters such as letters being ignored, expenses being paid very slowly or not at all. There needs to be a clear line of responsibility or, if shared, a clear indication of who is responsible for what in order to avoid confusion. Hence:

- there needs to be clarity over who is responsible for higher education at a policy level, including clarity of boundaries;
- wherever chaplaincy is placed in a structure, it needs to be resourced;
- it is critical to make clear who is responsible as the point of communication for higher education in each diocese, as chaplains often reported being outside the communications loop.

47 Concerning communication, chaplains often appeared to be omitted from one diocesan mailing or another, which can cause the loss of useful interaction with other areas of ministry. Chaplains often have contemporary experience of mission, adult education, youth, liturgy, etc. and can contribute much to a diocese. What do chaplains have to say to the Church, and how can it be said through the existing structures? The Church also needs opportunities to hear feedback from young adults, the students of our institutions.

48 Time-lapse between chaplain appointments is far more detrimental than in a parish, where an interregnum can be valuable for the congregation. In higher education, however, the message thus conveyed to an institution is that they are unimportant and that the Church lacks professionalism (it doesn't happen in Oxbridge colleges). In addition, important chaplaincy momentum can be lost, particularly with regard to student ministry. With approximately a third of students leaving each year, the personal link between a chaplain and a succession of students is of critical importance.

49 Admittedly there may be some difficulty generating sufficient interest for debate when chaplaincy is only a very small part of a diocese's ministry. However, some dioceses are working across diocesan boundaries to establish a critical mass and usefulness. Similar cross-boundary cooperation might be explored by dioceses with few higher education institutions. All dioceses would benefit from ongoing interaction with chaplains in order to hear the messages coming from people involved in education.

50 The nature of higher education institutions now varies far more, from the tradition of a residential campus environment to institutions having huge numbers of more locally based students of all ages. Different approaches to chaplaincy may be required thus demanding different support from dioceses. This may seem an obvious statement, but discussion at national conference suggests that chaplains are often facing some of these fundamental questions alone.

51 Another structural consideration in the diocese is having someone who understands higher education chaplaincy in the diocese to whom the chaplain can relate for:

- personal support – of the 'off-loading' kind;
- personal support – in terms of strategy and ideas.

52 Ecumenical posts in chaplaincy have differing arrangements. Diocesan support would be channelled through such local structures where they exist. However, the questions above apply as much to these appointments and their support structures as to dioceses. 'Sending bodies', whether Anglican or ecumenical, may not support higher education ministry well. As one contributor put it, noting church tendencies to change slowly, '(dioceses/Church bodies) haven't the faintest idea how to resource such creative ministry'.

questions of practice
chaplaincy and the wider Church

53 Consider how the wider Church may be in conversation with chaplaincy. Bring together a group to discuss, forward and promote chaplaincy in a locality (whether in a college, university, diocese, or region). Some chaplains are fortunate in this respect, but this is an ongoing aspect of chaplaincy, to question and develop a variety of work under the label of chaplaincy.

54 Discover those with understanding to be involved. Simply appointing an individual because they were a chaplain 20 years ago, or because someone is an academic, does not necessarily equip them for creative dialogue with a chaplain now. Where is the Church's expertise?

55 Explore partnership. Chaplaincy ministry may be enabled by a chaplain, not necessarily carried out solely by the chaplain but resourced by the wider Church. It is most important to recognize institutional boundaries and professional practice in this respect, but the chaplain can be a conduit enabling the wider Church to contribute constructively towards higher education ministry from the highly professional to the very practical:

- it is possible for lay Church members to meet with a few students to discuss realities of working in business or commerce;
- a retired bishop or other Church member beyond the university, given appropriate selection, might participate in occasional groups for a term considering applied theology, information technology, or ethics, for example;
- it was noted that some Church groups via the chaplain, in discreet cooperation with appropriate college staff, are providing food parcels for destitute students;
- students learning to fend for themselves are being offered cookery lessons by local parishioners;
- a Church college supplies a welcome goodie-box to all freshers, thanks to local churches.

chaplaincy and diocesan policy

56 Include college principals/vice-chancellors and higher education institutions in deanery visitations by the bishop.

57 Length of appointment is an issue that the Board has written to bishops about before. It necessarily takes about three years for a chaplain to understand their institution and earn respect. It would be good practice at this three-year stage for the chaplain and bishop (or whoever appropriate) to decide on a clear run to perhaps seven years. Waiting until the end of a five-year contract to review matters can take the edge off a chaplain's focus, especially if they envision college initiatives that would take a few years to implement. It is foolishness to waste three years of investment by then allowing unnecessary uncertainty to distract a chaplain in their prime.
Far better for them to focus on a few years with purpose, without a constant eye on vacancies, when they have understood their institution well enough to make strategic plans for such a period.

58 It can be mutually valuable for a chaplain to have a regular meeting with their bishop, archdeacon or some other with higher education responsibility. One chaplain remarked, 'There is nothing to stop a chaplain emailing their bishop for a pub lunch' (the national officer would like to know if this ever happens).

59 Chaplains are in colleges on behalf of the Church as a whole. It is important for the Church and dioceses to own chaplaincy. It is equally important to prevent individuals trying to own chaplaincy in an unhelpful way. Healthy ownership finds expression in good communications and support in the partnership between chaplain and diocese; it is also expressed in good structures and practice.

60 The town and gown relationship is changing, and local community links with universities are now of utmost importance. Institutions are therefore seeking to break down barriers. The Church may play a positive role in this.

61 *Other faiths.* This matter is receiving the increasing attention of higher education institutions. In some institutions it is also an opportunity for Christians to demand fair treatment. This issue will have to be considered more by dioceses in future. Chaplaincies vary enormously in their response to this matter, sometimes depending on the attitude of the college involved or the outlook of the individual chaplain. Dioceses may need to increase their awareness of other faith groups in their local context.

chaplaincy and structures

62 Intensity requires breathing spaces. Chaplaincy work in certain periods is extremely intensive and most colleges/campuses never close. Out of term, chaplains sometimes have contractual agreements to fulfil which other clergy have no experience of, particularly chaplains placed within student services:

- Widespread introduction of semesters and modularization has radically restructured the academic year in many places.
- The popular image of long vacations does not now apply. Work beyond chaplaincy has to be kept in proportion and diocesan personnel realize that chaplains already have a full-time job, often with little support. Parish associations can vary in their helpfulness or be a hindrance.
- Careful thought must be given to avoid making excessive demands on a chaplain by diocesan or parochial attachments in order to avoid excessive fatigue.
- However, a realistic strategy and plan for the interaction and promotion of chaplaincy within a diocese remains vital.

63 Some cathedral attachments were reported to work well, as chaplains are part of a larger team where the congregation understands that such clergy are not directly involved in day-to-day congregational matters.

64 In contrast, some local church attachments (either the chaplain on the staff of a local church or the chaplaincy itself being formally attached to a specific parish congregation) can be counterproductive, as individual congregations frequently have false expectations of chaplaincy and can bring unhelpful agendas that cloud the overall work of chaplaincy. This rarely results in greater support for chaplaincy but more likely a dilution of chaplaincy and less presence in the college.

65 More than one chaplain reported having to undo an association with a particular church. This is not uncommon and raises questions about the proper purpose of such connections. Student attendance at churches is volatile and where such relationships with chaplains are made, they should be kept under regular review.

66 There may be a need to set up an alternative mechanism with a light touch, for diocesan higher education oversight (such as previously performed by sometimes defunct diocesan further and higher education committees) to compare notes, receive feedback from one another on issues and developments, and learn from the outcomes of new initiatives.

67 Some specialist chaplaincy advisory groups do not always function well. Is their purpose made clear and boundaries set? How is membership decided and renewed/retired?

68 Some ecumenical teams work well and have a clear structure or pattern to their work. Others are not well-founded or monitored. Provision is sometimes made for the national officer or local expert to act as consultant, but dioceses are sometimes unaware or unsupportive financially of such possibilities. The Anglican Church must be aware of the 'out of sight out of mind danger'.

69 Local advisory groups can be most energizing, but some are not always helpful, especially if their members do not understand chaplaincy ministry. Being a member of college staff is no guarantee of usefulness for membership. How might chaplaincy supporters be better selected and briefed?

70 It is essential to provide formal chaplaincy representation and feedback into diocesan structures.

71 Higher education chaplains might usefully interact with others in diocesan ministry, for example in following up the recommendations of *Youth Apart*, given the large number of young adults in education.

72 If processing expense claims is too time-consuming for the diocese, why not devolve responsibility for the management of the appropriate budget to the chaplain along with a member of college staff supportive of the work?

73 An unusual possibility, if appropriate, is the example of a students' union president accompanying a chaplain to address the local/diocesan synod on the realities of student life. They do not have to be a churchgoer themselves to be included in this way. (In fact it is good for an outsider to encounter the Church in a listening context.)

chaplaincy support

74 Is a safe arena available for discussing issues raised by the higher education sector, questioning hard and asking the unthinkable?

75 There is a question of sensitivity in diocesan support due to the varying levels and its effectiveness. Some chaplains report 'better none than misplaced support'. This is hardly commendable practice.

76 The national officer encourages chaplains to pay careful attention to their support, but is at a distance. Who, locally, can care for chaplaincy and its chaplains; and what might be seen as interference rather than support?

77 At one venue, the phrase *blub and blab* was received with some amusement and aptness. A chaplain requires different types of support and these must not be confused. Trust and chemistry are factors in this. What works for one chaplain may not work for another. Sufficient support might be received from structural meetings. Spiritual direction, however, might rightly be external to the diocesan structure. Some flexibility and sensitivity are required in the matter of support, but it cannot be assumed that it is taking place without appropriate interest being taken by a diocese.

a breadth of resources

78 *Using existing resources to the full.*

Dioceses can encourage their chaplains to utilize the chaplain network, especially the programme of national events, to develop their ministry:

- annual professional conference/convention in September;
- consultation for recently appointed chaplains in January;
- Church college chaplain residential in March;
- strategic ministry review consultation in July;
- training days.

79 The value of sector events is the importance of continually exploring theological aspects of chaplaincy and promoting appropriate forms of ministry to changed higher education institutions; as one chaplain put it, 'to clarify one's calling and be focused, not simply loitering with intent, a model that is 20 years out of date'.

80 Dioceses can encourage chaplain attendance of the sector events by providing funds for the consultation for recently appointed chaplains and the annual September events in particular, often held by the Board of Education with ecumenical partners.

81 Chaplains reported 'Essential support for ministry in the fast-moving context of higher education', concerning their involvement in the national network. Additional ministerial support may include provision of a work consultant, regular ministerial review, peer review, visit of national officer, chaplaincy team development process, etc. Other aspects of support may simply happen or be set up by the chaplain or diocese.

joining in works both ways

82 Learn to use to full potential existing structures, such as:
- diocesan committees, synods, deaneries and chapters;
- national higher education conferences, chaplain training days, national/diocesan officers;
- college staff training, chaplaincy management bodies.

83 Dioceses can join in the fray. As well as being crucial to professional development and continuing higher education awareness as a chaplain, the national chaplaincy events may also be useful for diocesan personnel. Not only do dioceses need to resource and encourage their chaplains to attend, but also, periodically, to send representatives of their diocese to increase diocesan understanding of the sector and its support.

84 Non-chaplain participants of the consultations themselves were most positive about these opportunities to meet and discuss chaplaincy issues. Other such regional gatherings or discussion of chaplaincy in deaneries, synods and other forums may therefore prove valuable.

85 The purpose of visits by the national officer may be simply for personal support, or used creatively as a spur to bring people together who might not normally meet: from luncheon with the vice-chancellor and other senior officers, to discussion with Christian staff and students.

communicate, communicate, communicate

86 Communicating more widely:
- are chaplains on all appropriate diocesan mailing lists?
- is chaplaincy in the diocesan prayer cycle?
- does the bishop receive a regular prayer letter, or similar information from chaplains?
- are parishes aware that chaplains are working in challenging circumstances on their behalf?
- has chaplaincy been featured in diocesan newspapers or parish magazines, etc.?
- thinking through links between diocesan, parish and chaplaincy web pages.

87 How are all chaplains to receive clergy mailings (such as on *Common Worship*), when not included on the clergy payroll?

88 It is wise for chaplains, with others as necessary:
- regularly to review all college and student literature/intranet information, and the profile of chaplaincy within them;
- to likewise review diocesan literature, prayer cycle, etc.

This might be an appealing project for students.

89 Always make use of chaplaincy events, especially visiting speakers, for photo opportunities and reports in students' union, staff and diocesan newspapers/magazines.

chaplains on chaplains

90 New bishops require briefing on their local higher education context. It may help if chaplains are proactive in this respect.

91 Create opportunities for chaplaincy, institution and Church links (and be sure to write them up in diocesan newsletters):
- A new bishop can be invited to visit the university and have lunch with the vice-chancellor, as well as visit an academic department and hear a presentation from students' union officers. Making best use of such by involving the university photographer, internal news, etc., this also gives profile to the chaplaincy and to the Church's concern for education.
- The chaplaincy might host a variety of events, from chapter meetings or Mothers' Union visits, to a youth open evening on student life. You name it . . .

92 Chaplains can make good use of college staff training, often at no cost, to extend their skills and make contacts with academics. Valuable use can be made of induction courses for new lecturers.

93 Some chaplaincies include laity in their ministry teams. If chaplaincy is so crucial, request more hands on deck.

94 Consider the impact of communications technology on student lifestyle, and the new possibilities afforded by web pages, mobile phones, text-messaging, on-line conferencing, etc.

95 Host a termly lunch with people from the various student service areas: welfare, health, counselling, study support, hall wardens, students' union, etc. (This may be the only opportunity these people ever get to meet together!)

96 Consider establishing a termly lunch with the vice-chancellor/ pro vice-chancellor.

97 Arrange a regular formal meeting with the dean of students; a useful two-way information process.

98 Attend inaugural/public lectures, held in the college. Extend an invitation to diocesan personnel.

This higher education section report is necessarily selective. More detailed information of material contained herein or other instances of practice may be obtained from: paul.brice@c-of-e.org.uk

one question

If there were only one question . . .

Bishops
Am I supporting chaplaincy in my civic role and telling its story during my visits to the Church that provides it?

Chaplains
Am I using to best effect the available gifts and resources of the wider Church in the chaplaincy endeavour?

Christians in higher education
'What is there to have faith in' in my institution and who might help articulate this?[5]

Communications officers
Do I see higher education chaplaincy alongside parochial ministry as an equal partner in the mission of the Church in the day-to-day outworking of diocesan communications?

Diocesan officers
How can I share a creative vision for chaplaincy ministry amongst colleagues and the diocese?

Parish priests
How can I encourage those in higher education to bring their issues of concern into the life of the parish?

Theological educators
How might chaplaincy ministry and formation training interact to enhance the Church's ministry?

appendix 1
background to the consultation process

This consultation arose out of a letter sent out from the Board of Education's Further and Higher Education Committee to all dioceses enquiring about their support for chaplaincy and chaplains in further and higher education. The resulting picture gleaned from this exercise showed that diocesan support was most varied, and sometimes patchy, and that we would do well to facilitate wider attention being paid to it: for the sake of the large number of people involved in such institutions and ministry to them, but also for the Church, as a body, not to lose touch with an essential part of its own work, which evidence suggests can become isolated and unsupported.

Hence, the project developed into a nationwide consultation of six national meetings held in Birmingham, Bristol, Durham, Liverpool, London and Sheffield. Nearly 150 delegates contributed, including people in the following roles: chaplain (from both further education and higher education), dean, lecturer, welfare officer, tutor, further education staff worker, bishop, archdeacon, DDE, DYO, AEO, director of training, DBE member, further education officer, General Synod member and Further and Higher Education Committee member.
The delegates included representatives of other Churches including: Methodist, Quaker, Roman Catholic and ecumenical representatives. Gratitude is extended to those who attended and also to those who hosted consultations.

The resulting consultation revealed much interest, energy and vision for this work. It is hoped that this enthusiasm might be shared across the dioceses to encourage further consideration of how to have in place effective support mechanisms for this ministry. Also, that such support evolves to meet the demands of the fast-changing education sectors, which will continue to see substantial changes in succeeding years.

The report is intended to be read widely: theological training circles, chaplains, deans, bishops, archdeacons, CMEOs, DDEs, DYOs, AEOs, directors of training, DBE members, further education officers, General Synod, Further and Higher Education Committees, Archbishops' Council.

appendix 2
diocesan responses to original Further Education and Higher Education Committee letter of enquiry

summary and observations

1 *What is the current diocesan structure for further and higher education sector ministry as a whole?*

2 *What support structures for chaplains are currently in place?*

Replies were at variance in answering questions 1 and 2 on structure and support. The formal structure was often interpreted as a support mechanism so that the differentiation was blurred.

There is no common structure across dioceses for the structuring and support of further and higher education chaplains ('amorphous', was the reply from one diocese and that was only describing its own). Further education, higher education or further and higher education committees or 'groups' sometimes exist, particularly in dioceses with well-established education chaplaincy. One diocese is reorganizing into three mission teams of which chaplains will be a part. A number of dioceses are grappling with changing their structures and support in response to institutional changes in the sector in their area. A small number of dioceses rely on the diocesan bishop or a diocesan officer for the support of chaplains with little other formal support or specialist committee deliberations.

Higher education sector ministry, presumably due to its long history and relatively high number of full-time chaplains, seems to have a more recognized structure within dioceses than further education. Additional support, in terms of financial and committee structures, may be in varying states of repair. (When discussing this at the recent higher education chaplain conference there was a distinct impression from chaplains that, whilst formal structures may exist, recognizable support is not always felt. This may be a pastoral matter but nonetheless requires addressing.)

Further education sector ministry, with very few chaplains employed full-time, seems to have attracted less attention in the past, but support structures have often existed, commonly in conjunction with higher education. There have been several recent examples of diocesan further education oversight appointments which it is hoped will develop further education ministry in the dioceses concerned, sometimes spilling over into a neighbouring diocese.

Regarding support, this was sometimes 'encouraged', but often left to a chaplain to set up. A few dioceses encouraged attendance at national events. One cannot help but get the impression that some diocesan support is notional.

3 *To what extent are colleges/universities contributing towards the funding of chaplaincy in your diocese?*

A small number of institutions contribute directly to chaplain salaries, sometimes funding their entirety, but generally salaries are met by dioceses with contributions by way of premises, office services, budget or secretarial support. Housing is usually undertaken by dioceses, although there are examples of institutional housing, usually with some associated campus duty. Some dioceses reported an increasing financial contribution towards chaplaincy but, equally, other institutions had reduced their contribution due to financial stringency. (Chaplains with teaching responsibilities impact upon financial arrangements.)

4 *What significant changes or trends have you detected in diocesan chaplaincy provision over the last 10 years and what new creative partnerships have evolved?*

A variety of trends were reported, but no common pattern observed. Duplicated comments included the increase in ecumenical cooperation within chaplaincy, the increasing openness towards chaplaincy in further education and increasing multi-faith cooperation within higher education. One point made was the huge increase in student numbers and the importance of chaplaincy in the Church's mission, particularly regarding young adults who might otherwise not come across the Church at all. Another remark was that institutional cooperation and attitude to finance so often depended on the personalities in an institution and their perception of chaplaincy.

5 *There are moves towards regional planning of further education and higher education. Are you aware of any in your region and how is the Church involved in these initiatives?*

Very few reported any significant regional cooperation, although there was some regional awareness that might develop. Two responses referred to Lifelong Learning Partnerships and two instances reported were the situation created by universities taking on colleges across a wide area, sometimes from the further education sector in another diocese.

In conclusion, a handful of dioceses have a vibrant structure, which is very often fuelled by an active forum for discussing issues amongst chaplains, academics and diocesan officers. This is often accompanied by deanery, synod, or open events with a focus on further and higher education ministry. Other dioceses have the potential for such a forum or activity but might require an injection of new vision and creative facilitation. A handful of dioceses have little higher education activity within their boundaries and find it difficult to maintain any significant diocesan interest in higher education issues. Further education institutions are more evenly spread across the dioceses compared to higher education, but ministry sometimes lacks any coordination at diocesan level.

There is a strong case to be made for each diocese to review how it might best support and facilitate further and higher education ministry, which could include consultation with chaplains, academics, diocesan officers (such as Diocesan Education and Youth Officers) and local churches in an effort to determine pertinent issues and good support practice. A key aspect would have to be discovering where in the local church other interested parties are to be found. A good forum for the meeting of minds would not necessarily require a great deal of funding.

The Revd Paul E P Brice
Secretary, Further and Higher Education Committee
Board of Education
Originally dated September 1999

notes

introduction

1 *Anglican World* noted some years ago that education is a global business. What issues does this raise for a worldwide communion?

2 'I think the Church has to recognise that the variety of ways of learning are more pluriform than the ones it has traditionally engaged in; to provide a variety of situations, some of which are for people who will only have had basic education but some who have had the highest of education and are capable of handling concepts and principles in ways which the Church has not usually traditionally used in its teaching.' Prof. Walter James, Open University, General Synod workshop transcript 1996.

3 '. . . because this is such a recent experience, we have not yet adjusted properly – in terms of our perceptions of higher education and, wider still, our whole academic mentality. To put at its simplest, we act mass but think elite . . . we still make assumptions about the purposes, structure, content, outcomes of higher education that are more appropriate for an elite system.' Prof. Peter Scott, Vice-Chancellor, Kingston University, keynote lecture, 'New meanings of higher education' at the Anglican Higher Education Chaplains Conference, *Double Vision: Meaning, Message, Mission*, 4 September 2000. A full script is available at http://www.cofe.anglican.org/about/education/hefe.html

findings

1 A small working party is arguably more efficient than a formally constituted committee of considerable size, as long as it disseminates its work and does not become secretive. Such a group would consider how best to facilitate addressing educational issues including the following:

- where is further education and higher education discussed in our diocese?
- what are the current higher education and further education issues:
    a) of national interest?
    b) of local interest?
- how do these impinge on the work of the Church of England?
- how can addressing these in the diocese be energized?
- how might we therefore drive forward:
    - further and higher education committee or equivalent?
    - developing a higher education and/or further education interest group?
    - occasional open meetings or lectures?
    - chaplain local/regional gatherings?
    - chaplaincy/educational issues for debate/information in synod and elsewhere?
    - regular news from chaplains for parish/diocesan news media on a rolling basis?
    - joining with neighbouring dioceses in creative action on any of the above?

notes

2 Chaplaincy can sometimes be a severe culture shock for those not prepared for it, and requires informed support.

3 A workshop at national conference addressed this (with purple presence) and concluded that good chaplaincy and good parochial ministry were not dissimilar. However, chaplains still felt their formation training had left them unprepared; the root of this was that they were now learning to be chaplain to a whole community, not simply priest to a congregation. The former includes the latter, but not always vice versa. This, sometimes subtle difference, is not always fully understood as formation training rarely seems to provide any experience of this at conceptual level nor in practice.

section 2

1 See also *The Way Ahead: Church of England schools in the new millennium* (GS1406), 3.11 and 9.28ff. (these quotes may also be found on www.cofe.anglican.org/about/education/hefe.html).

2 A response to an email query on support:

> On Fri, 24 Sep 1999 The Revd Paul E P BRICE wrote:
>
> \> ─────────────────────────
>
> \> 1. What is understood by the term 'support'?
>
> \> 2. Where would it normally come from or be sought?
>
> \> 3. How might it be lacking?
>
> \> 4. Why might it be lacking?
>
> \> 5. How do we redress this?
>
> \> 6. What principles might be established to develop and measure support?
>
> \> N.B. There is often confusion/ambiguity regarding management structure (which can be supportive) and 'support', which is why I am seeking clarity in Q1 above.

notes

> A chaplain replied:
> _____
>
> Personally, I think these are appropriate questions and very important: there is a lot of misunderstanding (and a bit of stigma) about the notion of people in ministry needing support, instead of it being recognized as important for all of us and a constructive provision to enable people to perform their job better. My own perception is that 'management' in chaplaincy is both ambiguous and unhelpfully done; it is either seen as making sure you keep a close eye on the other person or leaving them entirely to their own devices. In contrast, 'supervision' can be constructive and enabling, and in the interests of developing potential. Because of the ambiguities of management I believe chaplains need to find networks for support, often beyond the job, but I don't think this should mean that dioceses etc. abrogate their responsibilities. Chaplaincy of all kinds does seem to fall outside of diocesan awareness. It is important that, as those licensed by the bishop, we are known by the bishop and involved in regular ministerial review. I hope some of that is helpful.

3 The 'fluidity of being church' refers to the increasingly varied manifestations of the Church, of ministry (e.g. chaplains in shopping malls, chaplains to clubbers) and different patterns of gathering (or not gathering, for those finding Christian support via electronic communication). In this context a number of chaplains would refer to: Leonard Sweet, *AquaChurch: Essential Leadership Arts for Piloting Your Church in Today's Fluid Culture*, Central Publishing inc, Loveland, Colorado, 1999. 'Liquid Church' was also the title of a seminar given to chaplains in 2001 by Pete Ward, see www.cofe.anglican.org/about/education/hefe.html

4 See note 2 in the introduction above.

5 The way that I define the task of a chaplain is: they are there to pose the question to the university, and indeed to the Church that puts them there, what is there in higher education to have faith in? That is a question that people can use a chaplain to think with and about. Anybody can use a chaplain for those ends, you do not have to be a Christian believer. The question then is how, in practice, does a chaplain set about raising the question of, what is there in the institution to have faith in, in the broad sense that I mean?

I think myself there's a threefold process. The first thing that a chaplain has to do is to show an interest in the place and find out; to pay attention to the agendas that are at work in the institution and to the faith that is in it. Therefore, the chaplain doesn't bring a prefixed agenda of his or her own, but has to pay attention. That is something that is quite hard to do and involves visiting round the place, and generally finding out.

The second thing that happens, and comes out of going and finding out, is that people in the institution begin to draw the chaplain into certain questions that they have themselves concerning the life of the institution and the values that are at work in it. These are not necessarily Christian people. Very often Christian people are the slowest to see the point of working like this. The fact is if you show interest in the institution, what the joys and the frustrations of working in such a place are, you will find that people may well use you to precipitate certain questions that are around which they have on their minds, but which they have no particular easy way of articulating in the everyday life of the department they are in. They can either do it as individuals or they do it collectively, and you find yourself involved in some sorts of projects that may take several weeks, or several months, with particular parts of the institution – looking into the questions that lie behind the questions that are the everyday business of that part of the university.

The third thing that comes out once you are involved in the life of the institution, trusted, and have taken part in it in different places, is that it is possible to bring to bear your own perceptions and judgements, to set up questions that occur to you from your own point of view and your own traditions, and to raise them with men and women of goodwill and to pursue them. I have been surprised at the extent to which many busy and important people in their own spheres, will actually take up and make available the facilities to pursue the questions that are raised by the chaplain in a life of the institution, and in these ways, over a period of time, it is possible to raise the question of, 'what is there in the institution to have faith in?', to produce some sort of answer, and perhaps to begin to be part of the difference that makes there be things worth having faith in, in the institution.

The Revd Tim Jenkins, Dean and former chaplain, from transcript of chaplaincy video, *Being there* . . . Further extracts are available from:

www.cofe.anglican.org/about/education/hefe.html

index

academics
  and attitudes to chaplaincy 18
  interaction with xi, 30
  and local churches 21
accountability x, 5, 20
Adult and Community Education Services 2
adult education 1, 2, 4, 7, 21
Adult Learning Inspectorate 4
apprenticeships, modern 2
archdeacons, and support for chaplains 24
Association of Colleges of Further Education 4

bishops
  and civic connections xiii, 19, 31
  as college governors 7
  and deanery visitations 24
  and links with higher education 19, 20
  retired 24
  and support for chaplains 29, 33
Board of Education
  Further and Higher Education Committee ix, 7, 32
  and higher education chaplaincy 15, 21–2, 28

change
  in Church 14, 18, 23
  in education ix, x, xi, xii–xiii, 14–15, 16–17, 20–21
  in society xii
chaplaincy
  and diocesan structures 7–8, 9–10, 11–12, 21–3, 26, 33–5
  diocesan support for ix, x, 11, 12–13, 19–20, 23, 24, 27–8, 31, 32, 33–4
  ecumenical provision 5, 7, 10, 23, 26, 28, 34
  funding for 18, 20, 28, 34
  institutional attitudes to ix–xi, 17–18, 19–20, 34
  and institutional structures 25–7
  management of 14, 20, 28
  models and approaches to 17, 23
  multi-faith 5, 11, 25, 34
  ownership of 24–5
  resourcing x, xi, 12, 22, 23
  reviews of 15, 27
  as stakeholder in higher education 17
  and the wider Church 23–4
chaplaincy advisory groups 13, 26
chaplains
  and cathedral attachments 25
  and changes in education ix
  and expenses 22, 26–7
  full-time x, 4, 33
  and gaps in appointments 12, 22
  as governors 6
  isolation of 18
  and job descriptions 3, 20
  and length of appointment 24
  and parish attachments 4, 25–6
  part-time x, 4, 12, 20
  and professional development 27, 28
  recently appointed 27–8
  and residentials 27
  role in further education 5–6
  role in higher education 16, 17, 21, 33, 38 n.5, 39 n.6
  and sector events 27–8
  supervision of 12
Christian Unions 6
Church of England, and change 14, 18, 23
Churches' Beacon Award for Sustainable Community Development 4, 10
Churches' National Adviser in Further Education 3, 7, 22, 26, 27, 28
citizenship 4, 5
clergy
  and changes in higher education 20–1
  and links with further education 4–6

41

index

and preparation of the young for higher education 20
and professional development x, xii, 27, 28
colleges, further education
  and higher education provision 1, 2
  independence of 1
  and vocational qualifications 1
colleges, theological x, xiii, 8, 31
committees
  diocesan 14, 26, 28, 32
  equal opportunities 6
  inclusive learning 6
communication
  in dioceses x, xiii, 8–9, 13, 21, 22, 29, 31
  and new technology 30
community
  and further education x, 1, 2, 4–5, 10, 12
  and higher education 19, 25
conferences xi, 11, 20, 27, 28, 33
congregations
  and links with further education 3–4, 6
  and links with higher education 21, 23–4, 25–6
Connexions Partnerships 4, 9, 11
courses
  distance-learning 4
  full/part-time 2
  modular 2, 25
culture
  changes in xii
  customer-centred 16
curriculum
  in further education 1
  values in 5, 10, 16

dean of students, interaction with 30
deaneries 27, 28, 35
deanery visitations, and higher education institutions 24
diocesan directors of education 7
diocesan synods 27
dioceses
  and communications x, xiii, 8–9, 13, 21, 22, 29, 31
  and engagement with education xiii, 7, 16
  and further education advisers 7, 9, 11
  and further education policies 8

and higher education chaplaincy reviews 15, 27, 28
and higher education issues 18–21, 24–5
and higher education policies 22
pressures on 14
recommendations to xii–xiii
and regional cooperation 18, 22, 34
and strategic planning ix, 5
structures 7–8, 9–10, 11–12, 21–3, 26, 29, 31, 33–5
and support for chaplaincy ix, x, 11, 12–13, 19–20, 23, 24, 27–8, 31, 32, 33–4

ecumenism, and provision of chaplaincy 5, 8, 10, 23, 26, 28, 34
education
  changes in ix, x, xi, xii–xiii, 14–15, 20–21
  and consumer culture 16
  mass provision 16
  and multi-faith issues xii, 18, 25
  recreational 2
  vocational 1–2
  see also further education; higher education
employability 2, 17
employers, and changes in education ix
ethics, in higher education 24

Foundation degrees 2
funding of chaplaincies 18, 20, 28, 34
further education 1–13, 33
  and diocesan structures 7–8, 9–10, 11–12, 34
  examples of practice 7–11
  full- and part-time courses 2
  and learning and skills sector 1–3, 7
  and the local congregation 3–4, 6, 35
  numbers in xii, 1
  and OFSTED inspection 4
  and policy-making 6, 8

governors
  bishops as 7
  chaplains as 6
  graduates, recent 16, 20–21

42

index

higher education 14–30
　changes in 14–15, 16–17, 20–21
　and diocesan structures 21–2, 26, 29, 31, 33
　and funding of chaplaincy 18, 20, 28
　issues on 16–17
　and multi-faith issues 18, 25
　numbers in xii, 14, 17, 34
　and regional cooperation 18, 22, 34–5
housing for chaplains 34

inclusion, social 3, 4, 5
information technology
　and further education colleges 4, 10, 13
　and higher education 24
inspection
　of chaplaincy services ix
　of further education 4
institutions, and attitudes to chaplaincy ix–xi, 17–18, 19–20, 34

James, Walter 36 n.2
Jenkins, Tim 39 n.6

laity see congregations; lay ministry
language, new x, 5
lay ministry
　and further education 6–7, 11
　and higher education 24, 30
learning
　recreational 2
　vocational 1–2
learning, lifelong 1, 9
Learning and Skills Council (LSC) 1, 4
Lifelong Learning Partnerships 35
Local Learning Partnerships 10
Local Learning and Skills Councils 10, 11
Local Strategic Partnerships 11

Methodist Church, and further education chaplaincy 3, 7, 10
ministry
　and future directions xii–xiii, 17, 31
　lay 6–7, 11, 24, 30
　and professional development x, xii, 27, 28
　to recent graduates 20–21
　reviews 27, 28

mission, and chaplaincy x, xi, xii, 4–5, 15, 21, 34

National Ecumenical Agency in Further Education 3
National Further Education Officers' Advisory Network 7
New Deal provisions 2, 4

officer, national 3, 7, 22, 26, 27, 28
OFSTED, and further education 4

parishes
　and engagement with education xiii
　and future directions of ministry xii
　and links with further education 3–4, 6
　and links with higher education 21, 23–4, 25–6, 31
parish profiles 13
　and support for chaplaincy x, 25–6, 29
pastoral care
　in further education 5, 10
　in higher education 24
planning
　diocesan ix, 5
　regional 3, 11
policies
　for further education 6, 8
　for higher education 22
prayer, for chaplains 11, 29
principals
　and attitudes to chaplaincy ix
　and diocesan structures 8, 9, 10, 19, 24

recommendations xii–xiii
regions, strategic planning 3, 11
retreat houses 12
retreats 10
Roman Catholic Church, and Lifelong Learning Officer 3

St Matthias Trust 9
St Peter's Saltley Trust 8, 10
Scott, Peter 36 n.3
skills, development of 1–2, 4
society, inclusive 3, 4, 5
spirituality, new understandings of 5, 9, 18
staff, college
　and attitudes to chaplaincy ix–x, 19

43

and changes in education ix
and chaplaincy advisory groups 26
Christian 4, 6–7, 21, 31
pastoral care for 5
training events for 10, 28, 30
see also academics
student services 30
students
  attendance at local churches 26
  and changes in education ix
  local awareness of 27
  pastoral care for xi, 5, 17, 24
students' union president 27

theological colleges
  and further education placements 8
  and future directions for ministry x, xiii, 31
theology xi, 15–16, 28
  applied/contextual 21, 24
town/gown relationships 19, 25
training, for chaplains 27, 28, 37 n.3

universities
  and funding of chaplaincy 18
  and local communities 19, 25, 36
  and role of higher education 18
  see also higher education

values
  in further education 5, 6, 10
  in higher education 16, 39 n.6
values, institutional ix
vice-chancellors
  and attitudes to chaplaincy ix
  and diocesan links with 19, 24, 29, 30

work, and human identity 5
workplace
  chaplaincy in xi, xii
  witness in xii, 6, 21
  and workforce development 2, 4
worship
  in further education colleges 6, 11
  and young graduates 20

young adults, interaction with xii, 15, 22, 26, 34
young people, and preparation for higher education 20
youth work 9, 11, 12, 21